Thinking and Writing About Art History

SECOND EDITION

Donna K. Reid

PRENTICE-HALL, Inc. and **HARRY N. ABRAMS**, Inc.

ISBN 0-13-022358-1

Printed in the United States of America

contents

part I: the study of art history

part II: researching and writing in art history

part III: model student essays

part I: the study of art history

preface

Thinking and Writing about Art History is designed to provide you with the tools to be a successful student of art history. In the past, professors tended to concentrate on the content of introductory courses, leaving discussion of methodology for courses taken later by art history majors. With the new emphasis on critical thinking, however, college professors have become increasingly conscious of the need to instruct their beginning students in the methodology of their disciplines, to teach students how to ask questions and how to answer them. Memorization has traditionally played a large role in art history courses, and most professors will still require you to memorize at least some significant works. This book is not concerned with that. Instead, my intention in writing the book is to help you to function as an art historian functions--to ponder the "givens" in the subject and to seek new insights, in reading an art history text, in discussions, and in your written work.

what is art history?

Simply put, art history is the study of works of art in their historical context. You can visit a building, view a work in a gallery or museum, or look at a reproduction in a book and respond to it, but an art historian thinks that is not enough. To an art historian, a work of art has a background, a history, and knowing that history enriches our experience of the work.

Art history could also be defined as what art historians create. Like any historical account, it is, in a sense, invented by people; it is an intellectual construct. Art historians are committed to discovering the truth, but know that the facts are not all available and those that are will remain open to interpretation.

Art history as a discipline in colleges and universities began about a hundred years ago. Art historical writing did exist prior to that time. One finds accounts of the work of an individual artist (as early as in ancient Greece), or statements of theory, such as the lectures of Sir Joshua Reynolds in the eighteenth century, or criticism designed either to evaluate works or to re-create a work verbally, such as Walter Pater's nineteenth-century description of the *Mona Lisa*.

Art history as such is usually said to have begun with the writings of a sixteenth-century painter, Giorgio Vasari, who wrote an account of the lives of artists, rich in biographical anecdotes. Another pivotal figure in the development of the history of art was Johann Winkelmann who, in the eighteenth century, wrote *Thoughts on the Imitation of Greek Art in Painting and Sculpture* and *History of Ancient Art* which introduced the modern art historical method of describing and classifying works of art on the basis of style. Nineteenth-century art historians tended to view art as evolutionary, their thinking influenced by Darwin's work in biology as was so much historical thought of the time.

Twentieth-century thinking in art history has been primarily concerned with the interpretation of works of art, with understanding what characterizes a work, the output of an artist, or the art of a historical period. Modern art historians are concerned with the choices which artists make and how those choices have changed over time.

Most art historical writing employs a scientific model: one of posing a question, advancing a hypothesis, gathering evidence, and drawing conclusions based on the evidence.

Just as scientists have come to recognize that they bring to their research a paradigm, a set of expectations that so far has been workable, art historians are now conscious that they approach research with habits of thinking derived from their experience in the discipline, with a sense of appropriate questions and appropriate answers. The challenge to art historians is recognized as not only being one of evaluating the worth of evidence and of accepted truths, but of standing back from their own work to query their working methodology.

why study art history?

You have signed up for a course in art history, very likely your first. You will have your own reasons--perhaps you have traveled and found museums or historical buildings interesting; perhaps a friend recommended the course or the professor; you may need to fulfill a humanities requirement for your degree.   What value can you hope to receive from an art history course? I wish here to speak from my own experience.

I value the fact that art history is one of the most interdisciplinary of all disciplines. I enjoy the wide-ranging fields of knowledge which can be brought to the subject or delved into while seeking answers to art historical questions--literature, philosophy, religion, psychology, economics, science, history, sociology, and even mathematics. Some examples of topics which have drawn on other disciplines: the relationship between the mathematics program in the Florentine schools in the Renaissance and the development of linear perspective; Masaccio's choice of Christ paying taxes as a subject for a painting commissioned by a family supporting the institution of an income tax; the influence of technology on art in the first decade of the twentieth century; similarities between T. S. Eliot's technique in his poem "The Wasteland" and the techniques of Cubism; the influence of Sigmund Freud's theories on the Surrealist movement.

Each of us has only our own experience, limited in time and place and by our perceptions and habits of thought. The visual arts, like all of the arts, give us the opportunity to share in the experiences of others, experiences that may be distant from us in time, or which in fact we would never want to experience in actuality, or experiences that we have in fact had but which we failed to attend to.

Our daily lives are filled with routine, and a great work of art is able to jerk us out of the ordinary, to open to us powerful human experiences. Standing for the first time in front of a work of art which you have thought about, discussed, written about, can be very much like that moment when you fall in love: an intense moment, a memorable moment to look back on with joy.

We are surrounded by art--on television, in magazines and books, in museums and galleries. You may have had the experience of learning a word, and seeing it in print over and over again, or of learning the name of a plant, and then truly seeing it for the first time. Familiarity with art is much the same: knowledge gives us a context, a focus.

The continual richness of mankind's artistic tradition gives me confidence in humanity, confidence in our creativity, our dedication to excellence, our dedication to shaping order out of the chaos of our experience.

Beyond the content of the course and the wonder of experiencing works, you will be enriched by the process of thinking and writing in the discipline. You, like an artist, will be involved in a creative act.

formal elements and principles of design

Typically an artist begins with a **subject** (what the work is about) (unless the work is to be a non-representational piece). After determining his intentions and what he wishes to convey about the subject (the **content**), he then makes choices about **form**--what the work will look like. The form of a work of art is analyzed in terms of the formal elements and the principles of design.

FORMAL ELEMENTS:

The formal elements are: line, shape, light and dark, mass and volume, color, space, and texture.

Line:
> Edges of shapes (contour lines)
>> or
>
> Strokes which indicate surface texture
>> or
>
> Compositional lines--the actual or implied lines that the viewer's eyes follow or that are indicated by the action
>
> It is helpful to describe the line characteristics in a piece: vertical, horizontal, diagonal; long or short; smooth or jerky; thick or thin, and so on.
>
> Lines serve to define shapes and surfaces, to move our eyes, to join and to separate, and to create mood.

Shape:
> Shape refers to a flat area (which may or may not have a defined contour line).
>
> ...A positive shape is a shape formed by one object or a group of objects.
>
> ...A negative shape is the shape of the void between objects.
>
> ...A biomorphic shape (such as one sees in the work of Joan Miró) is one that resembles the flowing contours of an organism.
>
> ...A geometric shape is regular (circles, triangles, squares etc.).
>
> Shapes create mood, suggest space if overlapped, and create pattern when repeated.

Light/Dark:

> 1) an artist may use a light source in a work (for instance, a candle or lantern depicted in a painting, or an implied source of light outside the painting which illuminates objects) or may design a three-dimensional work so that light affects it (using, for example, a shiny material like stainless steel or creating deep folds in the drapery).
>
> 2) may refer to ***Value*** (also called ***Key***): lightness or darkness. For example: A work might be described as having high value--painted in light colors; another work might have a strong contrast of value (for instance, pinks and dark reds, or black and white).
>
> Light and dark can be used to clarify form, to direct your attention, to create an emotional response.

Mass:

> An object has mass when it is perceived as having weight.

Volume:

> An object has volume when it is perceived as taking up space.

Color:

> In the late nineteenth century, artists and scientists developed a standard color theory which is still used to describe an artist's use of color.
>
> Definitions:
>
> *Hue*--a word used in the art field to describe a particular color. What, in common language, we might label as different colors (for example, pink and red) are, in fact, the same hue.
>
> *Value*--the lightness or darkness of a color. One hue has numerous values, ranging from high (light) through medium to low (dark).
>
> *Intensity* (also called *Saturation* and *Purity*)--the brightness or dullness of a color. A bright color is high intensity; a dull color, low.
>
> *Primaries*--red, yellow, and blue (the pigment colors which cannot be made from other colors)
>
> *Secondaries*--orange, green, and violet (each secondary color is made from two primary colors)
>
> *Intermediates*--each is formed from the mixture of a primary and a secondary color
>
> *Monochromatic*--one hue which is varied in value and/or intensity
>
> *Analogous*--closely related colors

Warm Colors--colors we associate with fire and sunshine: reds, yellows, oranges

Cool Colors--colors we associate with water and sky: blues, greens, violets

Colors are used
1. to create space (usually warm colors advance and cool colors recede)
2. to create mood
3. to convey ideas through symbolism
4. to draw the viewer's attention

Space:

Spatial depth can be suggested in a two-dimensional work (one done on a flat surface) in a variety of ways:

- overlapping
- changes in value
- placement in the picture plane (lower = closer; higher = farther)
- size (larger = closer; smaller = farther)
- color (warm colors usually advance; cool colors recede)
- *atmospheric perspective* (or *aerial perspective*): objects in the distance appear less detailed and the colors are greyed
- *linear* (or *geometric*) *perspective*: a mathematical system based on the fact that lines receding away from the viewer appear to converge at one or more vanishing points

Texture:

Texture can refer to the physical surface of the work (that is, of the medium--the paint, stone, and so on) or to textures created or suggested by the artist which are labeled as:

simulated: meant to imitate something real
abstracted: derived from real textures
invented: made up by the artist

PRINCIPLES OF DESIGN

The principles of design relate to the composition of a work of art, to its organization, the arrangement of its elements.

The principles of design include:

balance	the weights are distributed properly; equilibrium is created
symmetrical balance	the weights on the left and right are the same and the focal point is in the center
approximately symmetrical balance	the weights on the left and right are essentially the same, and the focal point is in the center
asymmetrical balance	the focal point is on one side or the other, and the equilibrium is achieved by dissimilar means
focal point	the part of the composition that draws the viewer's attention
dominance	an element (or elements) has more importance in the work
economy	simplification; reduction to the essentials
rhythm	a flow throughout the work, created by repetition
proportion	relative size relationship between the parts
unity	everything is properly related
open	the composition moves outward
closed	the composition is arranged to move the eye inwards

purposes of art

Historians use the term purpose to refer to the function of a work--what it was made for, its use.

It is important to be aware of the original purpose of a work, especially since the works we encounter in museums or reproduced in books are far removed from their original settings of tombs, palaces, temples, churches, or homes.

Many purposes have existed for art and the purposes differ from one culture or time to another. Art has functioned, for example:

... to give the maker or owner power over that which is represented
... to be used in religious rituals, to be worshiped, or to inspire devotion
... to provide for the afterlife
... to commemorate or memorialize
... to assert power
... to glorify or honor an individual
... to record--a person, an event
... to decorate
... to protest
... to edify
... to demonstrate an artist's skills
... to challenge or shock the viewer
... to express the artist's self
... to communicate
... to give the viewer an aesthetic experience

selected materials and processes of the visual arts

This section includes a brief description of materials and processes which you are likely to encounter while reading textbooks. No architectural terms are included.   For more information, consult dictionaries or encyclopædias of art.

Drawing:
> silverpoint: a stylus made of silver is used to draw on specially coated paper; a chemical reaction occurs as a line is drawn

> pastels: sticks of a chalk medium mixed with pigments and a binder

> conté crayon: a compressed compound of a pigment and a binder; available in sanguine, white, and three grades of black

Painting:
> acrylics: paints made of plastics

> encaustic: pigments mixed with wax; applied hot

> fresco:
>> In *buon fresco* (true fresco) pigment (usually mixed with limewater) is applied to a layer of wet plaster; the paint combines chemically with the plaster.

>> In *fresco secco*, the pigments are combined with a binder such as oil, egg yolk, or wax and applied to dry plaster.

> gesso: a ground for painting made from such materials as plaster of Paris and glue

> gouache: (rhymes with "wash")--opaque watercolor

> oil paints: pigment mixed with an oil such as walnut or linseed oil

> tempera: pigments mixed with water and a gummy material such as egg yolk

> watercolor: pigments suspended in a solution of water and gum arabic applied to wet paper

Printmaking:
> In printmaking, the artist is able to create a number of originals (except in monotype). Artists' prints are not what we might normally think of as a "print"--that is, a reproduction, but are instead original works of art.

relief processes: that which is not to be printed is cut away from the block (think of a rubber stamp). Two popular types are woodcut and linocut.

intaglio processes: in intaglio, the design is cut into the plate. When the plate is inked, the ink stays in the lines and is wiped off the surface of the plate.

engraving: the lines are created by pushing a burin, a sharp metal tool, across a metal plate.

etching: the metal plate is coated with a waxy resist, lines are drawn through the resist, and then the plate is dipped in an acid bath which eats into the exposed areas of the plate.

drypoint: a metal plate is drawn on with a pointed needle which leaves a burr, a ragged edge; this results in a soft line when printed.

aquatint: the plate is covered with a porous ground and then dipped in acid. The resulting surface will print in different values depending on the density of the ground. Line may be added in etching or drypoint.

mezzotint: the plate is textured with a tool called a rocker; the texture (which would print as a solid black) then can be smoothed away to achieve higher values.

lithography: a printing process developed in the late eighteenth century. The artist draws on a prepared stone with a waxy crayon; the stone is then wiped with a mixture of nitric acid, water, and gum arabic. When ink is applied to the stone, the ink adheres only to the crayon.

silkscreen (serigraphy or screenprinting): a stenciling process in which cloth is stretched on a frame, areas which are not to print are blocked out, and then ink is pulled across the fabric using a squeegee and is printed onto paper laid underneath the stretched fabric. Each color is usually printed separately.

monotypes: a transfer process where pigment or ink is applied to a surface such as glass or Plexi-glass, paper is laid on the surface, and the paper is rubbed to pick up the color.

Sculpture:
 additive: materials are added together (as in modeling and assemblage)
 subtractive: material is removed (as in carving)
 modeling: the use of a malleable material such as clay or plastic which can be manipulated
 casting: a liquid material is poured into a mold
 assemblage: a construction using found objects
 relief: a term for sculptural forms which remain connected to a background
 freestanding: works which can be viewed from all sides (in-the-round)

describing style

STYLE

Style is defined as the characteristic manner employed in works of art. Style is determined by the choices artists make about purpose, medium, technique, use of formal elements, and subject matter. Art historians speak of the style of a period (for example, Gothic), a movement (such as Impressionism or Cubism), or an artist.

ARTIST'S INTENTIONS

Many art historians feel that their role is to understand the intentions of an artist, based on whatever historical evidence is available to them.

It is easy to confuse the terms *purpose* and *intentions,* but the difference can be useful. Purpose refers to the function of the work. The term *intentions* is used in discussing the artist's goals in the piece: what has the artist sought to do, what challenges has he set for himself, what is she seeking to work out?

For example, artists might explore the possibilities of a new medium, seek to incorporate "real materials'" into a painting (as in collage), emphasize the surface of the canvas while at the same time creating deep space through color, or create drama through lighting.

ARTIST'S APPROACHES

A number of terms are used to characterize an artist's approach to his work, terms which are helpful in understanding changes in styles in the history of art.

Terms used in describing an artist's approach to depicting reality:

Conceptual:　　the artist finds his subjects in the world around him and depicts them as he *thinks* of them (not as he *sees* them)

Representational: any of a number of approaches which have to do with the way something is seen

Illusionistic:　　a convincing imitation of the appearance of objects in the world

Naturalistic:　　an approach which suggests fidelity, not so much to appearance, but to the being of something

Realistic:　　usually carries the connotations of a frank look at everyday reality

Idealistic:　　the world is represented as better than it actually is

Stylized:　　representation according to conventions rather than in a fashion based on seeing

***If there is little or no resemblance to the perceived world, a work may be described as*:**

Abstract (or Abstracted):　　　the artist begins with the real world but does not seek to imitate its appearance

Non-Representational
(non-objective):　　　the artist does not relate his work to the appearance of objects in the world

Other terms used to describe style:

Classical and Romantic: cultural historians describe an artist as having a "habit of mind" which either prefers a composition which is orderly, closed and static, and symmetrical (the classical) or prefers a composition which is less orderly, is open and dynamic, and is asymmetrical (the romantic).　Within one stylistic period, artists with both approaches may be working: Michelangelo and Raphael in the Renaissance, Van Gogh and Seurat in the Post-Impressionist period, Matisse and Picasso in early Modern, for example.

Baroque: the name of a historical period which has been generalized for use as an adjective meaning dramatic, exuberant, active, emotional

Impressionistic: the name of a historical period which is used been generalized for use as an adjective to describe a technique which is brushy and spontaneous

Expressionistic: used to describe a style in which the artist's strong emotions distort line, color, forms

selected glossary

Most art history textbooks will have a lengthy glossary which you should consult as you are reading. This is a list of terms which may have meanings peculiar to the discipline or which may present difficulties. For stylistic terms, see **describing style** pages 11-12. For terms used to describe form and design, see **formal elements** pages 4-6 and **principles of design** page 7. For technical terms, see **selected materials and processes of the visual arts** pages 9-10.

academic: adhering to the rules of an "academy"--a school which teaches strict, usually conservative rules

allegorical: figures or objects exist solely for the purpose of conveying an abstract idea: Truth, Beauty, Justice, Liberty, Rome

calligraphic: rhythmic, expressive lines or brush strokes

canon of proportion: a system to determine relative sizes (often of parts of the human form)

cartoon: a full-sized preparatory drawing

chiaroscuro: an Italian term which refers to a contrast of light and dark areas which create an illusion of mass and space

content: the meaning of the work, the message which the artist wishes to convey

foreshortening: in a two-dimensional piece, objects (such as an arm) which appear to come toward the viewer must have the dimensions adjusted (that is, shortened)

form: is used in three ways: 1) to describe what the work looks like (the use of color, texture, value etc.) 2) the shape of an object 3) the overall appearance of a work

golden section: a canon of proportions based on the ratio of two parts of a whole in which the smaller of the parts relates to the larger as the larger relates to the whole (AB/BC = BC/AC); often used in architecture to determine the proportions of a building or in a composition to determine placement of objects/figures

iconography: the study of subject matter (often religious subjects such as "the representation of the Madonna in 14th century Italian art" but also non-religious subjects: "dogs in Renaissance portraits," "insects in seventeenth-century Dutch still lifes"

modeling: has several meanings: 1) in sculpture, the use of a malleable material such as clay or plastic which can be manipulated 2) in a two-dimensional piece, the use of lights and darks to create a form that appears three-dimensional 3) posing for a work *monumental*: grand, impressive, often large-sized

painterly: a term introduced by Heinrich Wölfflin in his book *Principles of Art History* which suggests an approach that utilizes shifts in tone to define forms.

plane: a flat surface

picture plane: in a two-dimensional work, the surface of the piece. Objects may be described as lying in the picture plane or receding behind it

plastic: as an adjective, means having a sculptural, three-dimensional quality

portrait: a representation of a real person, living or dead; a likeness of the person

purpose: why a work is done; the function or destination of an artwork

sfumato: "smoky"--describes the blending of tones in a painting to produce an atmosphere which seems to veil the figures

subject: what the work is about

symbolic: an object has two layers of meaning: it is itself (a flower) but it also stands for an idea (for example, purity).

tenebrism: very strong contrasts of light and dark, with the darkness often pierced by a bright beam of light; used primarily to refer to Baroque works

interpretative approaches in art history

Richard Schiff, in his introduction to *12 Views of Manet's Bar*, notes that ". . . art historians assume that every work of art has a plan, order, procedure, or motivation to be uncovered, described, and analyzed--whether an individual's willful intention (conscious) or a society's ideological construction (unconscious)." He adds, "To put meaning and order into art--to operate beyond merely finding what is already clearly there--constitutes the art historian's task; what he or she has been trained to do" (11).

Many interpretative approaches exist in current art historical thought. Among them are:

...   viewer response--how does the viewer respond to the piece and how has the artist caused that response?

...   analysis of the intentions of the artist

...   formalism--the study of the use of the formal elements and principles of design and the resulting aesthetic effect

...   iconographical--the study of subject matter and content

...   biographical--the study of the life and career of an artist; how a work of art relates to the artist's life

...   study of techniques

...   study of sources and documents

...   stylistic analysis

...   cultural--how does the work reflect the culture that produced it--its religion, philosophy, science, and so on

...   sociological and Marxist criticism--works of art as reflective of social factors such as patronage, class, economics

...   feminist--concerned with issues of gender: attending to the role of women artists; examining how women artists construct their world--what subjects do they choose and how do they represent those subjects; considering the depiction of women in works by male artists; examining the effect of the gender of a viewer on his or her experience of a work.

...   semiotics (the study of signs)--originating in the study of language, semiotics is now also applied to images with the notion that a work is "read" and the viewer must de-code and uncover hidden meanings. A work of art is a fiction, an invention, and may not mean what it appears to mean.

...   deconstructionism--meaning is open rather than "given"; assumptions about a work must be questioned; every "answer" leads to a new question (so ultimately, nothing is knowable).

...   psychoanalytic--searches for the unconscious mind underlying the imagery of a piece; assumes that the artist did not *know* what he or she was doing in the piece and that the artwork may be the result of pathological drives.

art criticism

Art historians tend to see their role as differing from that of critics: historians interpret the work and seek to understand its place in the culture that produced it, while critics, in addition to interpretation, evaluate works of art and seek to convince their audience of worth or lack of value.

Criticism does, however, have its place in the history of art. The perceived quality of a work affects its inclusion in textbooks and in art shows or museums; historians will often write on works that are for them powerful and moving; writing on contemporary works whose place in history is not clear is often evaluative (and you may find yourself writing critical essays on recent artworks); criticism from the time of an artwork is often useful in understanding the work's place in history.

Criteria used in evaluating the effectiveness of a work change over time, but twentieth-century critics tend to bring some of the following expectations to a work. The work should:

1.   Catch the viewer's attention
2.   Cause an emotional response; impact the viewer
3.   Be innovative, original, creative
4.   Show effective use of the medium
5.   Give evidence of technical skill
6.   Show successful use of principles of design
7,   Show successful use of elements of form
8.   Fulfill its purpose
9.   Have a message, something significant to say
10.   Show that the artist had clear goals
11.   Change our view of the world
12.   Be a memorable image
13.   Reward repeated viewing

part II: researching and writing essays in art history

---

the topic

---

thinking about a topic

When you write an art history essay, you first should choose a topic--one that is *narrow* enough for the assigned paper and one that *needs to be investigated.*

Weak essays often have too broad a topic--photography, the Egyptian pyramids, Rembrandt. In each case, you would have to narrow the subject. For instance, Rembrandt > Rembrandt's paintings > Rembrandt's religious paintings > Rembrandt's *Supper at Emmaus.*

Effective essays will answer a question--one to which the answer is either controversial or not agreed upon. You should not merely summarize information which is readily available.

Essay assignments may or may not require research in sources. In either case, your intention in an essay is to bring your own thinking to the question you have posed. If you do use material from sources, it should be used to advance your explanation or argument.

finding the topic

Some ideas: Look back through your text for artworks which you have particularly enjoyed or have been puzzled by. Look through your class notes; professors often mention research possibilities. When you have a subject area in mind, do preliminary reading to help you to narrow your topic. You may find interpretations or statements that you disagree with or which seem incomplete to you, or you may discover aspects of the topic that seem worth pursuing.

posing the question

Art historical topics tend to fall into four categories: questions of style, questions of iconography, sociological questions, and interpretations of a work. In posing your question, you might consider the following (remembering that a good question is a narrow question, one that will lead to a thoughtful and thorough answer):

Style (see pages 11-12)

> What is characteristic of a given style?
> How does one style differ from another style (a previous or contemporary style)?

Iconography

> How is a subject depicted by an artist or during a particular time?
> How did the representation of a subject change?

Sociology of Art

> How are works of art reflective of social factors such as patronage, class, gender?

Understanding and Analyzing a Work of Art

1. The basic facts about the work:

   What is the title?
   When was the work done?
   Where was the work done?
   What medium was used?
   What is the work's size?

2. What is the subject of the work?

3. What is the purpose of the work? (see page 8)

4. What is the content of the work (the artist's message)?

5. What period or movement does the work belong to?

6. What choices did the artist make concerning the formal elements and the principles of design? (see pages 4-7)

7. What is your response to the piece? How did the artist's formal choices affect your response?

8. How does the work fit into the artist's career?

9. How does the work fit into the artist's life?

10. Did the artist use sources--either literary or visual?

11. Are there any contemporary written documents pertaining to the work--either by the artist or by others? (contracts, letters, biographies, autobiographies, criticism etc.)

12.   What is the work's relationship to the world view at the time it was created: religion, politics, economics, science, mathematics, psychology, sociology and so on?

13.   What was the public and critical reaction to the work in its own period?

14.   How does the work compare to earlier works or to works being done at the same time?

15.   What was the process of the piece? Do written documents exist that help to illuminate the process? Did the artist use models? Do preliminary sketches or paintings exist?

16.   What is the significance of the piece?

17.   Is the work symbolic?

an example of finding a topic

You have an assignment to write a six-page paper for an art history class on modern art and have identified the work of Picasso as an area of interest. It is necessary to narrow the subject of "Picasso" down to a workable topic for a paper of that length. The process of narrowing the topic might be from The Life of Picasso > The Paintings of Picasso > Early Paintings by Picasso > Picasso's Cubist Period > *Les Demoiselles d'Avignon*. After some preliminary reading, you discover that entire books have been written on *Les Demoiselles d'Avignon*, so the painting is too broad a topic for a fairly short paper. After doing further reading and looking at *Understanding and Analyzing a Work of Art* (pages 19-20), you identify several aspects of the painting which would be interesting to research:

1.   How does the work fit into the artist's life? (Some scholars state that the content of the piece reflects Picasso's difficulties with women.)

2.   What was the process of the piece? (Numerous preliminary sketches exist.)

3.   How does the work compare to Matisse's *The Joy of Life*? (Picasso suggested that *Les Demoiselles d'Avignon* was a response to the Matisse painting.)

4.   How does *Les Demoiselles d'Avignon* reflect the thought of the time? (You saw a video that suggested that the development of modern art may have been influenced by Einstein's Theory of Relativity and by Freud's theories on the interpretation of dreams.)

5.   How does the work fit into Cubism? (The painting has long had the reputation of being the first Cubist work, but you read that some scholars are now questioning that idea.)

locating information

sources

In writing an essay, you may need to locate source materials for information or illustrations.

You should investigate the resources available to you in the library and on the Internet. Remember that reference librarians are trained to help you in your search.

You will want to be familiar with:

1.	Locating books
2.	Locating media such as videotapes, slides, laser disks
3.	Locating articles in periodicals
4.	Locating reviews of books
5.	Using reference books, especially
	...	general reference books such as encyclopædias and atlases
	...	art reference books such as dictionaries, handbooks, and encyclopædias
	...	religion and mythology materials
	...	biographical materials
	...	historical materials
6.	Borrowing materials from other libraries
7.	Locating information on the Internet

search strategies

library materials

When you search card or computer catalogs and periodical indexes, you need to identify subject headings that will get you to the material. Generally you start narrow and then broaden the search as necessary.

For an artwork, for example, try the title of the work and then the artist, and then broaden to the art of a century, period or movement, city and/or country of origin, museum or collection, media. Try a combination such as Sculpture--20th Century; Art--Italian Renaissance. Try rearranging the terms. When you locate a book in a library catalog, look at its subject headings and try those. When you have located a book, encyclopædia article, or periodical article, look to see if it includes a bibliography.

It is best to keep track of subject headings that you have used in searching a source. Later, in another source, you may discover another possibility; you can return to previous sources to try the new heading.

In using bound periodical indexes, such as *Art Index* and *The Readers' Guide to Periodical Literature*, begin your search with the most recent years and go back five or perhaps ten years. Online periodical indexes usually list articles from several years.

Internet

For searching on the Internet, you will utilize search engines, programs which run searches for you. It is worthwhile to use more than one, since they are not the same. You should spend time learning what some search engines do and how they work.

Some to try are:
        http://www.itools.com/find-it/find-it.html
        http://www.eblast.com/ (the Encyclopædia Britannica Internet guide)
        http://www.isleuth.com/ (keyword search on multiple search engines)
        http://www.highway61.com/ (a meta-search search engine)
        http://www.infohiway.com/
        http://www.excite.com/ (organizes search results by summary)
        http://www.infoseek.com/Home?pg=ultra_home.html
        http://www.altavista.digital.com/ (searches over 31 million pages)
        http://www.lycos.com/
        http://www.yahoo.com/
        http://www.metacrawler.com/ (searches several search engines)
        http://www.webcrawler.com/

The search engine will usually give you a list of Websites to look at--some of which will be relevant to your search and others which are not. Once you have found a useful Website, you should add it to your personal list for easy access (look to see how your Web browser does this).

A special feature of searching on the Internet is that Websites will often indicate *links* to other Websites. You are likely to feel as though you have no direction as you follow link after link, but remember that you can click *back* and find your way back to a particular site.

evaluating sources

Whether you are using print sources or online sources, you want to be sure that the source is considered appropriate for research. There are a number of ways to do this. In the case of a book, you may be able to locate a book review (which should be by a reputable author). Look in periodical indexes for a listing of a review and also consult *Book Review Digest*. In addition to reading any available reviews, for print sources you should consider the following:

    1.   Date of publication (in art history, older sources are often still useful, but it is helpful to have current sources as well)

2. Author's credentials (degrees, affiliation with an institution of higher education)
3. For articles, look at the magazine and its audience--is the magazine scholarly? Popular? Reputable?
4. Bias of the author (does it appear that the author has approached the subject objectively?)
5. Does the author's research appear to be based on reputable sources?

Websites are particularly difficult to evaluate since anyone can put information on the Internet. As with print materials, you must try to assess the credibility of the source. Museum Websites and educational institution Websites may well be the best sources for you. Your instructor may also suggest Websites. Some Websites are reviewed by the Encyclopædia Britannica staff at http://www.eblast.com. Top humanities Websites are listed at <edsitement.neh.gov>. Computer magazines may recommend Websites and you can find selected sites listed in *Art on the Internet 1999-2000: A Prentice Hall Guide*.

recording information

From the beginning of your research, write down source information on 3 x 5 cards (not on pieces of paper or in your notebook). Cards make alphabetizing your final list of sources easier.

A bibliography card for a book should have:

1. author's last name, first name, and middle initial
    a. unless the author is known by her initials
    b. use the following abbreviations to indicate editor (ed.), compiler (comp.), translator (trans.)
    c. if there is more than one person responsible for the book, include all of the names
2. title of the book and subtitle
3. place of publication
    if you are seeking the information on the title page and there are multiple places of publication listed, choose the one that appears to be the most important (indicated by type face or size or placement on the page), or, if one is not distinguished from the others, choose the first
4. publisher
5. date   if you are locating the date from the book itself, look for (in order of preference):
    1. publishing date from the front of the title page
    2. publishing date from the back of the title page
    3. most recent copyright date (indicated by c. and the year)
    4. if there is no date listed, use the abbreviation n. d.
6. call number of the book (if known)
7. you may include other information such as which library owns the book or the date when you order a book from another library

Bibliography cards for periodicals and newspapers:

Different types of magazines require that different information by recorded. Be sure to write down the full title of the magazine, not the abbreviated title which is used in the indexes. "Journal" refers to scholarly periodicals (such as *The Art Bulletin*).

1.   For a magazine published weekly:
author, title of the article, title of the magazine, date (written day, month, year), and pages

2.   For a magazine published monthly:
author, title of the article, title of the magazine, date (month and year), and pages

3.   For a journal paginated by volume:
author, title of the article, title of the journal, volume number (in arabic numerals), year of publication, pages

4.   For a journal paginated by issue:
author, title of the article, title of the journal, volume number (in arabic numerals), issue number, year of publication, pages

5.   For a newspaper:
author, title of the article, title of the newspaper, date (date, month, year), section number, pages

Online sources vary considerably and the methods for listing sources are still changing. You should check with your instructor or librarian for up-to-date information or go to the MLA Website: http://www.mla.org>. Generally, you want to record the information which would allow someone else to locate the source and the date that you accessed the source.

1.   If the information has been published in print, record the standard information for that type of print source, the data base or Web page where you located it, the Web address, and the date you accessed it.

2.   If the information was written for the Internet and not published previously, write down the available information which may include author, title of the article, title of the Web page, date of the Web page, address of the Web page, and the date you accessed it.

For further information on what is to be recorded on bibliography cards, consult an English composition text or (depending on which citation style your instructor requires) look at the *MLA Handbook* (or <http://www.mla.org>) or at the *Chicago Manual of Style*.

taking notes

Regard note-taking as a *thinking* process, not a copying process. The aims of note-taking are:

1. to select information
2. to record where you located information
3. to categorize information for easy access
4. to put most of the information into your own words
5. to record quotations accurately
6. to record your own ideas in response to your reading

Each note (whether taken on a card or on paper) should contain the following:

1. source (it is easiest to give each source a letter on the bibliography card and then to use that letter on the note)
2. page number
3. a heading which identifies the content of the note
4. a note which is faithful to the original
5. when useful, your own comments (indicate your own ideas with double parentheses or square brackets)

Types of notes are quotation notes, summaries (condensations of a fairly large amount of material), or paraphrases (the idea restated in your own words).

Quotation notes should only be taken if you expect to use the quotation; the idea may be stated especially well, or you wish to include the exact wording of an authority.

The key to successful paraphrasing is to read the section, *look away* from the source, and write the note. This will insure that you have used your own words and that you have understood the idea. Then look back at the source to check the accuracy of the paraphrase.

writing the essay

thesis

An effective essay will explain something (exposition) or it will attempt to persuade the reader (argument). The essay should have a clear thesis which
     a)   states the topic
     b)   gives the writer's viewpoint about the topic
     c)   may suggest the points to be covered in the essay

The thesis is the *answer* to the question you posed about the topic.

introduction and conclusion

It is important that the introduction be carefully crafted to interest readers and to inform them of the subject of the essay.

Some writers prefer to include the thesis sentence in the introduction, while others prefer to close the essay with it.

The conclusion should bring the essay to a satisfying close. Take care not to stop before you have concluded and not to go on past the point where you have finished.

mechanics of an essay

1.   As with any college-level writing, the essay should be well organized, interesting, and correct in grammar, punctuation, spelling, and mechanics. Consult an English composition text if you need to review. Also see ***proofreading hints*** page 33.

2.   Titles of artworks are italicized (or underlined in handwriting and typing).

3.   Titles of periodical articles are put in quotation marks; book, magazine, and newspaper titles are italicized (or underlined in handwriting or typing).

4.   Copies of artworks are usually included with an essay. Label each one with a plate or figure number and refer to it by number in the essay. You should type the source onto the plate.

5.   Format of the essay: Use at least a one inch margin on the top, bottom, and sides of the page. Double-space the essay. Most professors will require that essays be typed in 12 point type. Use a title page or put your name, the course information, and the date in the upper right-hand corner of the first page. Number each page after the first.

the principles of using sources

In an essay, you need to make it possible for the reader to locate and read your sources.

You also must make it absolutely clear which ideas are yours and which come from sources.

Words or ideas which come from a source (book, magazine, etc.) and which can be identified as *belonging* to a particular person or group *must be credited* to the source. On the other hand, ideas which can be considered *common knowledge* among art historians need not have a source indicated (but if you are unsure about whether an idea is common knowledge, be safe and provide a source citation).

Failure to cite sources of words or ideas is considered plagiarism--that is, academic theft--and the consequences can be very serious.

For every idea in a paper, it must be clear whether the idea is yours or from a source. This means that you should signal the beginning of information from a particular source with a phrase such as "According to Henry Sayre, . . ." or "In the book titled *A World of Art*, Sayre says . . .". If you are weaving together information from several sources, your signal phrase might say something like "Scholars have interpreted the symbols in Van Eyck's painting in various ways."

Most of the material from sources (80% or so) should be paraphrased--put into your own language. Use quotations only if: they are worded especially well, you want to dispute them, or they are impossible to paraphrase. Furthermore, use a quotation only if you intend to comment on it, to consider its implications.

methods for citing sources

Professors of art history will usually require either the MLA system (in-text documentation) or the Chicago style (footnotes or endnotes) for citing sources. You should ask which your professor prefers. In either case, be sure to follow that particular method strictly; imitate the examples given below, and be sure not to mix up the citation systems.

MLA documentation style

in-text documentation
The essential notion of the MLA system is that the writer supplies in the essay whatever information is needed to locate the full bibliographic information in the Works Cited at the end of the paper. The necessary information, in most cases, is the author's last name and the precise page number where the information was found. Be sure that the source for any idea which is not yours is clear. Take care to imitate the punctuation, spacing, and underlining in the following examples. Note that "p." and "pp." are not used with page numbers.

If you mention the author's last name in your sentence, put the page number(s) in parentheses at the end of the quotation, paraphrase, or summary.

> Ken Shulman claims that Piero della Francesca's works are now being recognized as masterpieces (13).

If the author's last name is not mentioned in your sentence, put the last name and the page number(s) in parentheses at the end of the paraphrase, quotation, or summary.

> The artist Robert Rauschenberg has "a whale-sized appetite for seizing and recording imagery on canvas, paper, cloth, plywood and most recently on such resonant surfaces as copper and brass" (Dudar 54).

If you have more than one source by the same author, use a short form of the title.

> "As has been mentioned, Northern sculpture was virtually untouched by Italian influence up to the sixteenth century" (Panofsky, Early 76).

If you have a source without an author, use the first word of the title in the documentation (ignoring "A" or "The").

If you use a quotation over four lines long, it should be indented 10 spaces on the left and double-spaced. Do not use quotation marks. Put the documentation after the final punctuation mark.

the works cited

At the end of the essay on a separate sheet, include a list of works cited (that is, ones you used in the essay) alphabetized by the author's last name or the first word of the title if there is no author, double-spaced between all lines, with every line except the first of each entry indented 5 spaces. Note that the entries are not numbered.

The Works Cited on the next page provides a model for you to imitate (remember that you can consult the MLA Web page for the most recent information: <http://www.mla.org>).. Various types of sources are given as examples. Be sure to imitate the examples for your sources exactly. The Works Cited page which follows has been reduced and placed in a box so that explanations could be written in the right-hand column. Your Works Cited page should have Works Cited centered at the top and should be typed with normal margins. Do not put a box around it.

Works Cited

Dudar, Helen. "The Artist Who Wants to Embrace the

Whole World." <u>Smithsonian</u> May 1991: 54-67.

"Giotto Di Bondone." <u>Encyclopædia Britannica Online</u>.

19 Mar. 1999 <http://members.eb.com/bol/

topic?eu+37618&sctn=2#s_top>.

"John Singer Sargent." 14 Mar. 1999 <http://

metalab.unc.edu/cgfa/>.

Murray, Julia K. "What Is 'Chinese Narrative

Illustration'?" <u>The Art Bulletin</u> 80 (1998): 602-615.

Panofsky, Erwin. <u>Early Netherlandish Painting: Its Origins

and Character</u>. Vol. 1. New York: Harper & Row,

1971.

---.<u>The Life and Art of Albrecht Dürer</u>. Princeton, New

Jersey: Princeton University Press, c. 1955.

Russell, John. "The Cogency of Bridget Riley." <u>New York

Times</u> 28 January 1979, sec. II: 27.

Stevens, Mark. "Revival of Realism." <u>Newsweek</u> 7 June

1982: 64-70.

Tuchman, Phyllis. "Picasso's Sentinel." <u>Art in America</u>

86.2 (1998): 86 (11). Searchbank. 4 Mar. 1999

<http://web2.searchbank.com> .

monthly magazine

encyclopædia article-online

Website

journal paginated by volume

book (published in volumes)

book by the author listed above

newspaper article

weekly magazine

previously published article in a journal paginated by issue located in an online data base

Chicago documentation style

In the Chicago style, footnotes (at the bottom of the page) or endnotes (a list at the end of the paper)
are used to indicate quotations, paraphrases, or summaries from a source. A raised arabic numeral
is placed at the end of the material derived from a source. The note for each source provides publication
information about the work and the page number upon which the material was found. If a work is
repeated in successive notes, the Latin abbreviation "Ibid." may be used if the page is the same or, if the
page number is different: Ibid., page number.

The bibliography includes both works that you cited and those you consulted. Put it at the end of the
essay on a separate sheet, with the entries alphabetized by the author's last name or the first word of the
title if there is no author, each entry single-spaced with double-spacing between entries, all lines except
the first of each entry indented 5 spaces. Note that the entries are not numbered. Encyclopædias,
dictionaries, and the Bible are usually not included in the Bibliography.

in the text

In *American Painting,* Jules Prown remarks that "The most obvious fact about early

American painting is that there was so little of it."[1] He notes that little is known about seventeenth-

century painting since documentation is scarce and only about fifty paintings have survived.[2]

the notes (footnotes in this case, but the same format would be used for endnotes)

---

[1]Prown, Jules David. <u>American Painting: From its Beginnings to the Armory Show</u>
(New York: Rizzoli International Publications, Inc., 1987), 11.

[2]Ibid., 12.

Bibliography

Dudar, Helen. "The Artist Who Wants to Embrace the Whole World." <u>Smithsonian,</u> May 1991, 54-67.

monthly magazine

"Giotto Di Bondone." <u>Encyclopædia Britannica Online</u>. [19 March 1999]. Available from http://members.eb.com/bol/topic?eu+37618&sctn=2#s_top: Internet.

encyclopædia article--online

"John Singer Sargent." [14 March 1999]. Available from http://metalab.unc.edu/cgfa/: Internet.

Website

Murray, Julia K. "What Is 'Chinese Narrative Illustration'?" <u>Art Bulletin</u> 80 (1998): 602-615.

journal paginated by volume

Panofsky, Erwin. <u>Early Netherlandish Painting: Its Origin and Character</u>. Vol. 1. New York: Harper & Row, 1971.

book (published in volumes)

---.<u>The Life and Art of Albrecht Dürer</u>. Princeton, New Jersey: Princeton University Press, c. 1955.

book by the author listed above

Russell, John. "The Cogency of Bridget Riley." <u>New York Times</u>, 28 January 1979, sec. II, p. 27.

newspaper

Stevens, Mark. "Revival of Realism." <u>Newsweek</u> 7 June 1982, 64-70.

weekly magazine

Tuchman, Phyllis. "Picasso's Sentinel." <u>Art in America</u> 86, no. 2 (1998): 86 (11). [4 March 1999]. Available from Searchbank http://web2.searchbank.com: Internet.

previously published article in a journal paginated by issue located online

The Bibliography above provides a model for you to imitate. Various types of sources are given as examples. Be sure to imitate the examples for your sources exactly. The Chicago Manual of Style is vague on entries for online sources, but these appear to be reasonable. This Bibliography page has been reduced in size so that explanations could be written in the right-hand column. Yours should have Bibliography centered about one inch down from the top, be typed with normal margins, and be numbered consecutively with the paper. There should be no box around it.

an essay revision checklist

1.   IDEAS AND CONTENT: Is the essay clear in purpose and does it convey ideas in an interesting, original manner that holds the reader's attention?

      Is the content engaging, illuminating, ambitious? Do you demonstrate independent thinking?

      Is the topic narrow enough for an essay of the length required?

      Did the topic need to be investigated?

      Is there a clear thesis?

      Do clear, relevant examples and details develop the central idea?

2.   ORGANIZATION: Have you organized the material in a way that enhances the reader's understanding and that helps to develop a central idea or theme?

      Have you written an inviting introduction that introduces the topic and engages the reader?

      Is the conclusion satisfying? Does it bring the essay to an end without adding new material?

      Does each paragraph develop one idea?

3.   WRITING STYLE: Does the essay bear the stamp of an individual writer?

      Have you varied the lengths and types of sentences to avoid monotony and to achieve emphasis?

      Are the words chosen well? Have you avoided slang and informal language?

4.   SOURCES: If sources are used, are they properly cited?

      Is the Works Cited (MLA) or Bibliography (Chicago) done correctly?

5.   WRITING CONVENTIONS: Did you proofread the essay carefully, insuring that it is free of errors in grammar, spelling, punctuation, and mechanics?

      Have you observed the conventions regarding titles of artworks, books, magazine, newspapers, and articles?

proofreading hints

Proofread your essay carefully, paying particular attention to the following:

words that are often confused

1. accept/except: *accept* is a verb meaning "to receive"; *except* is either a preposition meaning "excluding" or a verb meaning "to exclude".
2. affect/effect: *affect* is usually a verb meaning "to influence"; *effect* is usually a noun meaning "result".
3. *all right* is written as two words.
4. *a lot* is written as two words, but should be avoided in formal writing.
5. too, to, two
6. they're, their, there
7. who's, whose
8. it's/its: it's = it is; its is the possessive pronoun.

punctuation

1. Remember that punctuation marks assist the reader by providing signals about what the reader is to do. Be sure that your punctuation does not confuse the reader. Try reading your paper out loud to check punctuation.
2. Do not connect two complete thoughts together with a comma (this is the error known as a comma splice). Instead you should make two sentences, or connect the ideas using either a semicolon or a coordinating conjunction (and, or, but, for, nor, yet, so) preceded by a comma.
3. Do not string complete thoughts together with no punctuation or conjunction (this is the error known as a run-on sentence).
4. Use a comma after an introductory clause. For example: After reading my text in art history, I understood linear perspective better.
5. Proofread carefully for possessives. Do not omit apostrophes which indicate possession. A common error in art history papers, for example, is saying "the work engages the viewers attention" where viewer's should be a possessive (the attention belonging to the viewer). But note that the possessive of *it* is *its* (as is the case with his, hers, theirs, ours, there is no apostrophe).

other common errors to watch for

1. Be sure that your pronouns have clear references.
2. Check to be sure that you have not written sentence fragments (incomplete sentences).

answering essay examination questions

Answering an essay examination question is in most ways similar to writing an essay. Some special considerations are:

1. Always be sure to write an introduction. There is a tendency to start an essay question answer in the middle. Be sure to identify what the subject of the essay is.

2. It is best to start an essay question with a thesis sentence in the introduction. This makes it clear to your professor that you have a clear point in mind, and it also helps you to organize the essay.

3. Do not assume knowledge on the part of your instructor (because then you will omit information that your professor wants to know that you have learned). Imagine that you are writing the essay to someone who is not familiar with the subject.

4. Your professor will be looking for specifics that support the point you are making. Be sure to include examples to illustrate your points.

5. Tie up the essay with an appropriate conclusion.

6. If the essay is not open book, you will not cite sources.

7. Many essay questions are comparison/contrast questions. There are two methods for developing comparison/contrast essays; decide which you are using before you write, and be sure to jot down an outline for you to follow.

    One method, called "subject by subject" is where you discuss one subject and then the other, being sure to include the same points in the same order.

    For example: the topic is to compare Michelangelo's Sistine Chapel ceiling to Raphael's *School of Athens*.

    Your outline is--

    1. Introduction including the thesis: Raphael's *School of Athens* and Michelangelo's Sistine Chapel ceiling, commissioned by Pope Julius II and done in the first decade of the sixteenth century, both reflect Renaissance humanism.

2.   Body of the essay:

Definition of Renaissance humanism

School of Athens
1. the historical background
2. the subject of the work
3. how the choice of subject and its depiction reflects humanism

Sistine Chapel ceiling
1. the historical background
2. the subject
3. how the choice of subject and its depiction reflects humanism

3.   Conclusion

The other method of developing a comparison/contrast essay is called "point by point." Rather than discussing one subject and then the other in the body of the essay, you work through the points you want to make.

Your outline is--

1.   Introduction including the thesis: Raphael's *School of Athens* and Michelangelo's Sistine Chapel ceiling, commissioned by Pope Julius II and done in the first decade of the sixteenth century, both reflect Renaissance humanism.

2.   Body of the essay:

Definition of Renaissance humanism

1. The historical background
   School of Athens
   Sistine Chapel ceiling
2. The subject of the work
   School of Athens
   Sistine Chapel ceiling
3. How the choice of subject and its depiction reflects humanism
   School of Athens
   Sistine Chapel ceiling

3.   Conclusion

part III: model student essays

Note: To conserve space, these essays are in 10 point type and single-spaced. Your essays should be in 12 point type and double-spaced.

a formal research paper (*MLA documentation style*)

Dorothy Thomson
Art 205
December 11, 199-

THE BURIAL OF COUNT ORGAZ

El Greco, born Kyrlakos Theotokopoulos, was a master artist when he created what I believe is the finest work of his career, *The Burial of Count Orgaz*. He was born in Crete which was part of the Venetian Empire, and he had traveled to Venice and studied with Titian and possibly Tintoretto. He went from there to Rome where he lived in Cardinal Farnese's palace. In Rome, according to Cowles, he bragged that they might tear down Michelangelo's *Last Judgement* and that he could redo it just as well, a statement that did not add to his popularity (70). He moved to Spain, it is believed, to gain the favor of the King, Philip II, but he failed in that achievement. In 1577 he went from Madrid to Toledo to work on an altarpiece. He spent the rest of his life in Toledo where his work was greatly appreciated and where commissions seemed to be plentiful, even when he was weak and ill in his last years.

In 1586, in Toledo, El Greco received a commission to paint a piece for the church of Santo Tomé. He signed a contract that agreed to the principal elements in the painting and that the painting was to fill the specified arch from top to bottom. Brown quotes the agreement:

> On the canvas, he is to paint the scene in which the parish priest and other clerics were saying prayers about to bury Don Gonzalo de Ruiz, Lord of Orgaz, when Saint Augustine and Saint Stephen descended to bury the body of the gentleman, one holding the head, the other the feet, and placing him in the sepulcher. Around the scene should be many people who are looking at it and, above all this, there is to be an open sky showing the glory of the heavens. (125)

Gonzalo de Ruiz, Lord of Orgaz, died in 1323 after a lifetime of charitable works. One of the bequests in his will was that the Church of Santo Tomé receive an annual donation to be collected from the citizens of Orgaz, a town under his domain, but, after 239 years, the town stopped making the donation. The parish priest, Andres Nunez de Madrid, sued the town to enforce the payment. He won his suit. The priest then decided to use the money to improve the burial chapel. He commissioned a lengthy inscription on the wall below the arch describing the miracle that had occurred at the burial of the Lord of Orgaz. He then petitioned for official recognition of the miracle which was granted in 1583; in 1586 he commissioned El Greco to paint the canvas depicting the miracle.

El Greco painted a magnificent canvas to fit in the designated space. The wall frames the approximately 16' by 18' canvas with a graceful arch and a dome above the area. El Greco combined what might be considered two pictures, showing citizens from the period, dressed in sixteenth century garb, priests and monks, the corpse of the Count and the saints holding him, portraying what might be a realistic funeral of the time in the lower half of the canvas; and in the upper half of the canvas he illustrated the saints interceding for the soul of the Count. He shows us Saint Peter and St. John the Baptist, angels and cherubim, and swirling clouds. He visualizes heaven for us. Brown says that a ninth-century funeral liturgy may have inspired El Greco's vision of paradise:

> May the angels lead you into paradise; may the martyrs welcome you on your arrival and bring you into the city of Jerusalem. May the choir of angels receive you and may you rest eternally. . . ." (126)

El Greco has dressed the body of the Count of Orgaz in a beautiful suit of armor and placed him just slightly off center in the lower portion of the canvas. The metal in his suit picks up the light. The saints at his head and feet are dressed in gorgeous brocade robes and the robes are embellished with illustrations. The lower skirt of St. Stephen's robe has a picture of the stoning of St. Stephen. St. Stephen is clothed and the pagans stoning him are nude. St. Augustine's robe has three pictures: each is of a single figure with a halo, possibly an apostle.

The priest at the far right wears a stole of brocade that is also decorated with miniatures.

The people at the funeral depicted in the painting were well-known figures in their time. The priest at the right in the brocade stole may be Andres Nunez de Madrid. It is thought that the face of the man with the mustache directly above the hand pointing skyward is a self portrait of El Greco. The boy kneeling to the left of St. Stephen is believed to be Jorge Manuel Theotokopoulas, El Greco's son, at about eight years of age. El Greco's close friend Antonio de Covarrubias y Leiva has also been identified as a participant.

The black dress of the period with the accents of the white collars, the gray robe of the monk, the white surplice of the priest, all magnificently contrast with the brocade garments of the saints and accentuate their glory. El Greco's funeral scene is calm and peaceful. It shows the dignity of intelligent, responsible men paying their respects to one of their peers. The figures are realistic and the scene appears factual. This scene points to the glorious, imaginative, and emotional scene above by the upward glances of the men with their feet on the ground.

El Greco lived in the time of the Spanish Inquisition and the Counter Reformation. Lassaigne tells us that Toledo was the ecclesiastic capital of Spain, with numerous churches, convents, and colleges (112). El Greco included two themes in this work that were important to the Counter Reformation. The Protestants professed that heaven could be obtained by faith alone or by Predestination, but the Catholic Church claimed that heaven could be obtained by faith and good works. The Catholic Church also believed in the divine intervention of saints. El Greco used the upper half of his art work to illustrate these Catholic beliefs. He combined the subjects of Jesus at the Last Judgment and the intercession of the saints for the soul of Gonzalo de Ruiz.

El Greco's paintings from this period on become more spiritual and more mystical. His style of painting human bodies that are long and thin comes from his intensely religious feelings. Diehl claims that

> . . . his disproportionately elongated characters, usually full-face with a quality of stillness and assurance in the midst of the most terrible circumstances, his almost uncanny sense for monumentality, his blazing lyricism of color, all proclaim that his debt to Byzantine art was much less sterile than has been thought. (18)

Lassaigne claims that the Byzantine influences in

El Greco's work were his method of preparing canvasses, his lack of depth in his paintings, and his foreshortening techniques (102). Other writers claim that El Greco's stylized bodies are a characteristic of the Mannerists. De la Croix said, "His elongated figures will exist in undefined space, bathed in a cool light of uncertain origin. For this, El Greco has been called the last and greatest of the Mannerists. . . " (707).

In executing his commission for the painting *The Burial of Count Orgaz,* El Greco fulfilled all of the stipulated requirements. To create his masterpiece he did more than that. He showed us life and death, heaven and earth. He orchestrated colors and light and shadows. He balanced figures and the composition while keeping to the required size, space, and shape. He played with our emotions and directed our religious beliefs. He depicted heaven within the strict Catholic beliefs of the Inquisition and still gave his imagination free rein. He painted portraits of himself and his contemporaries, Toledo's leading citizens, and had them complement the subjects of the work: the Count, St. Stephen, and St. Augustine. He flattered the church and the town with this masterpiece and it was sincerely done.

WORKS CITED

Brown, Jonathan. El Greco of Toledo. Boston: Little,

Brown, 1982.

Cowles, Gardner. The Story behind the Painting.

New York: Look Magazine, 1962.

De la Croix, Horst and Richard G. Tansey. Art

through the Ages. 7th ed. Harcourt, Brace,

and Jovanovich: San Diego, 1986.

Diehl, Gaston. El Greco. New York: Crown, 1967.

I.assaigne, Jacques. Spanish Painting from the

Catalan Frescos to El Greco. Geneva: Kira,

1952.

an art criticism essay

Kathleen L. Mrowka
Art 206
October 12, 199-

A Review of the James Rizzi Collection at the Augen
Gallery, Portland, Oregon

Rizzi's art is not for the serious or high-minded collector of great works. This collection merely offers a light-hearted view of the world through the eyes of an imaginative, optimistic local artist. Each of the nine paintings in Rizzi's display has its own unique theme, but Rizzi's recognizable and consistent style sets them apart from the other work in the gallery.

Even the most casual observer will immediately note Rizzi's unique three-dimensional effect. He achieves this by making a second set of the figures in the original painting and attaching them directly over the original figures with small foam spacers separating the identical forms. This would appear to be a tedious, time-consuming chore, but the effect is fresh and appealing.

Rizzi uses all of the primary and secondary colors to create his bright, cheerful compositions. He crowds his paintings with scores of crudely-wrought human and animal figures. These cartoon-like forms have undulating body lines with limbs like wet noodles that contort into impossible positions, creating a feeling of movement and happy intensity. In the zany party scene of *Let the Good Times Roll*, droll human figures of all shapes and colors pack a dance floor and cozy up to a bar at the foreground. An amusing little dog and cat are tucked into the tight composition too.

Rizzi's backgrounds contribute greatly to the overall impression of ordered chaos. In *Let the Good Times Roll*, he decorates the background with whimsical objects such as banana peels, beer cans, wine bottles, and crazy squiggles, swirls and spots galore. Rizzi's attention to detail and to the overwhelming numbers of figures and forms hold the viewer's interest after the initial attraction of his three-dimensional treatment. Whether his subject is the ghosts and goblins in *Trick or Treat* or people with umbrellas as in *Rain*, Rizzi is consistent in his merry depiction of life and fantasy. His goal is to make people smile--to lighten their spirits for a moment. There are no great messages. His art is not designed to challenge the viewer and could be considered somewhat superficial as a result. Rizzi appeals to the child in all of us that wishes for a safe, harmonious and happy world. James Rizzi's work is enjoyable, and he succeeds in his efforts to touch his viewers' emotions.

an informal response essay

Kelly Amsberry
Art 206
June 1,199-

Edward Lucie-Smith in *Art in the Seventies* calls Earth art, such as that of Christo and Robert Smithson, a combination of environmental art and Minimalism. Although practiced as "art" only in the late 1960s and early '70s, human attempts to reshape the landscape by our own hand are as old as our presence on earth. Robert Smithson's *Spiral Jetty* obviously refers to the creations of Native American Mound Builders, as well as to the similar contemporary practical structures such as the breakwaters common on our own coastline. (I think it is wonderful that *Spiral Jetty* has been covered by the rising waters of Salt Lake. This development adds a new dimension to the piece, showing the power of nature, and the transience of all things, both natural and man-made).

While I have not seen any of Smithson's work, I feel somewhat of a special affection for Christo's art since I was living in Sonoma County, California at the time he created *Running Fence*. This piece, made up of twenty-four miles of white nylon stretched across the bare hills near our town was a cultural, as well as a visual phenomenon. Christo said, in a 1981 interview with *Rolling Stone*, that in creating *Running Fence*, he wanted the people of our county to be "a part of his vision" and "bade them see and be a part of his art." As a teenager, I often participated in social outings that involved viewing Christo's fence, as it was being created, and again when it was completed. Most young people liked the fence from the beginning since it was strange and somewhat ridiculous, and especially because Christo had been able to build it in spite of opposition from the "authorities"--the local planning commissions, city councils, and some of the Italian farmers whose land it crossed. The *Running Fence* was big news in our small town from its inception, and everyone followed closely as Christo worked through his problems: acquiring permits, arguing with local bureaucracies, and finally creating and installing his fence. One issue I remember as an important one, although it is not mentioned in any of my reading, was the problem of how to get cows through the fence at milking time. The *Running Fence* was situated according to Christo's artistic vision, and did not take into consideration the practical concepts of dairy farming. Although this issue was the subject of great debate, I do not remember how the problem was solved!

Although Christo has said that the creation of his works is as much "art" as the finally completed piece, *Running Fence*, as well as being community entertainment, was a fascinating visual work. The miles of white fence were starkly visible against the grassland and the blue sky of northern California, and the fence seemed almost alive as it ran across the landscape. The angular forms were a fine contrast to the rounded hills of the area. From many sites we could also see the rounded very dark forms of the native Live Oaks silhouetted against the white: another effective contrast. The *Running Fence* took on still other qualities at night, as it rippled in the wind and reflected the moonlight.

Although Christo has been seriously (as I think rightly) criticized for his grandiose, obscenely expensive projects, the artist and his *Running Fence* provided an interesting insight into the nature of art for our community. It provided unavoidable exposure to art.

(Note that in this informal essay, formal citations were not required.)

three essays on the same topic

Gabriella Gyenes
ART 205
February 12, 199-

Giotto's *Lamentation*

The Florentine master, Giotto di Bondone, one of the earliest of the great Renaissance artists, painted a series of frescoes for the Arena Chapel in Padua of which perhaps the most outstanding is the *Lamentation*. The fresco could be considered a scene of immense grief if it were not for the kaleidoscope of colors, which outweighs the effects of the depicted tragic, human emotions.

The painting portrays an astonishing variety of ways in which individual grieving can be expressed. Giotto uses dramatic gestures, theatrical poses, and exaggerated facial expressions to convey what the final parting from the dead Christ, just removed from the cross, means to each and every figure. The mourners are mostly women, perhaps, because, by the nature of their gender, they are the ones who show their emotions more openly. Faces are becoming even more individualized in the Renaissance than they were in the Gothic, which can be noticed in the *Lamentation*. Human faces and hair are more accurately portrayed. Detailing has reached new heights with Giotto. Bodies are still well hidden under heavy drapery, but they have volume, mass, and they are rather well proportioned. The artist's limited knowledge in the field of human anatomy becomes obvious upon observing the unclothed body of Christ more closely.

Richness of color characterizes the *Lamentation*. The clothing, which appears to be a mixture of Classical drapery, Byzantine robes and contemporary attire, is executed in primary and secondary colors, varied in value and intensity. There is a sharp contrast between the solid blueness of the sky and the rich colors of the mourners' draperies which are repeated in the robes of the despairing angels fluttering above. This repetition of color unites the two sections--sky and earth-- of the painting. The placement of the angels provides the necessary weight for maintaining balance within the picture plane, which would just about topple over without them. Without their presence, the lower half of Giotto's work would be overly crowded, and the upper half bare. The use of gold is refreshingly restricted to the halos of figures and drapery borders.

There is no definable direction of a light source originating from the inside or outside the picture plane. We perceive an outdoor scene simply because the accessories, as limited and unrealistic looking as they may be, imply the presence of nature surrounding the group of people. The sloping, rocky, unnatural looking hillside slicing through the picture plane in a diagonal direction with its fairly straight line and monochromatic, neutral coloring corresponds in line and color to the body of Christ, and leads the eye downward to the scene unfolding in front of us. The implied gazes of the figures are also meant to direct the viewer's attention to the focal point of the painting, which is Christ.

There is still a strong linear sense in Giotto's style; his shapes are defined by sharp contour lines and outlines, yet his draperies have realistic folds with realistic shadows. For the first time since antiquity the flat surface of a picture gains a believable degree of three-dimensionality in Giotto's hands, which is achieved by overlapping, placement and modeling of figures.

The artist was successful in conveying the sense of tragedy, sorrow, and despair the followers of Christ must have felt upon his departure from this Earth. Giotto had taken the first decisive step toward the revival of interest in humanity, the expression of human emotions, and the magical creation of realistic, three-dimensional space on a two-dimensional surface--which was to become the triumph of the Renaissance.

Brenda Kellar
ART 205
February 13, 199-

Giotto's *Lamentation*

The beautifully disciplined, yet eloquently stated emotions of this piece is what first draws the viewer to it. The degree of restraint used to depict the emotional scene is what makes the viewer feel those emotions so deeply. This is not a scene that has been set with a heavy hand. It is a scene set with delicacy and control.

The colors used are soft pastels against a brilliant heavenly blue sky. These are not the colors associated with grief. Dark ominous heavy colors are normally used to portend sorrow, regret, and fear. In this case those emotions are beautifully stated in subtle shades.

The facial expressions of the subjects also project the emotion of the moment to the viewer. This is true of the angels as well as the mortals. Tears are not seen on any face. The impression the viewer is given is of resigned, accepting grief. The tears have all been shed and now the participants' grief is deeper and more personal.

The most eloquent emotive statements are in the body postures of the mourners. Mary carefully cradles Jesus' head in her arms. John flings his arms wide extending his body and bows his head over Jesus' body like an angel falling over him in protection. It is as though John wishes to dive into death, represented by Jesus' body, in order to follow him. Behind John are two apostles who show us a calmer, more accepting grief. They tilt their heads toward each other as though conferring on what to do now that the driving force behind their cause is gone. The woman standing behind Mary has her clasped hands raised to her cheek showing us the true grief felt by Jesus' followers at the loss of their shepherd. The angels each show us a different portrayal of sorrow, from gentle mourning to wild bereavement.

All of this emotion is illustrated by the position of the participants' bodies, from subtle gestures to agonized contortions. With this strong base as the skeletal structure of the scene, restrained use of color and facial expression brings beauty to this tableau. Anything less controlled and discerning would render this image exaggerated and inane.

Jessica Price
ART 205
February 10, 199-

Lamentation by Giotto

This fresco by Giotto looks different from anything I have seen so far in this course. What makes it stand apart is the incredible way Giotto has conveyed the sorrow and sense of tragedy felt by Christ's followers at his death.

The figures' facial expressions and body positions realistically portray the immense anguish they are feeling. The angels writhe in pain and agony. They each grieve in their own way. The center one's head is thrown back, his face distorted as if he were violently crying. Another covers his face with his drapery. Giotto succeeded in making all of the people complete individuals. The faces all express grief and yet they are different. The disciple John is doubled over in pain. Two other disciples look upon the scene with silence. Mary's arms are around Jesus and she has a look of concern and love for him. The women surround Christ, kneel down next to him, and gently hold on to his body. The way in which Giotto has communicated the despair of the situation is truly a great achievement.

What attracts me to artwork is how it makes me feel; what emotional reactions a piece of art can stir inside of me. This fresco makes me feel the sadness of the moment. It is very powerful in that way. It makes the death of Jesus much more personal and human. I mourn the death of Christ along with his followers. Mary is shown not only as a connection to God, but also as a mother holding her dying son.

The piece is breathtakingly beautiful and amazingly emotive. Giotto took the art of mural painting to a new level. The characters do not pose stiffly, but move with a realism new to frescos of the Middle Ages. Jesus' death is no longer just a Biblical story; it has become a real, and very sad, event.

Dorothy Thomson, *The Burial of Count Orgaz*

This is an explanatory essay which takes several approaches to the work: how the painting fits into the artist's career; the process of the painting; a description of the work; the relationship of the work to Counter Reformation Catholic thought; the style of the work (and its relationship to the Byzantine style); the achievement of the artist in the piece. The first paragraph is an overview of El Greco's career; the remainder of the essay is a close look at the painting itself. The conclusion includes the thesis and is an eloquent statement summarizing the paper. Notice that the student regarded the history of El Greco and of the painting as common knowledge. The quotations are few, but are well chosen: two are quotations of relevant documents; two are beautifully worded statements by scholars. The section on style is the weakest; it needed either to be integrated into the essay better or omitted.

Kathleen L. Mrowka, A Review of the James Rizzi Collection at the Augen Gallery

This essay was written after a visit to an art gallery to view contemporary art. The author's voice is lively and engaging and is perfectly calculated to match the exuberance of the pieces reviewed. The author has employed several critical criteria: the works are original, they catch the viewer's attention, the medium is used effectively, the work causes an emotional reaction.

Kelly Amsberry, Untitled

This essay is both enjoyable to read and informative. The author begins by considering the significance of environmental art. She then turns to *Running Fence,* sharing her personal experience of the work and including information not found in her sources. Her voice is both engaging and thoughtful.

Three essays on the same topic:

While the three essays vary in length (and therefore in amount of development), they are similar in a number of ways: all have a thesis in the first paragraph which sets up the essay; all show thoughtful reflection about the *Lamentation*; all concentrate on the emotional impact of the piece. The authors show their sensitivity to the achievements of the artist and their pleasure in the art of writing.

the author

Dr. Donna K. Reid holds degrees from Stanford University (Bachelor of English Literature), the University of California at Santa Cruz (Ph. D. in the History of Consciousness), and the University of Oregon (Masters of Library Science). She currently is a professor at Chemeketa Community College and Linfield College in Oregon, teaching courses in Art History, Art Appreciation, Design, and English Composition. Her interest in art history was awakened by a year of study in Austria. As a scholar, she specializes in the art and literature of medieval France. As a teacher of art history, her interest is in making art accessible to her students and in providing them with the means to think and write effectively in the discipline. From that interest has come this text.